Hours and Days

by
Kriti Mukherjee

Azalea Art Press
Sonoma | California

ISBN: 978-1-943471-48-5

Cover Design and Illustrations by:
Kriti Mukherjee

Dedication

To my loving grandfathers
Dr. Subhas Chandra Sen
and the late Swapan Kumar Mukherjee,
and my beautiful grandmothers
Indira Sen
and the late Debi Rani Mukherjee.

CONTENTS

I. Midnight

II. Dusk

III. High Noon

IV. Daybreak

I.
Midnight

Popsicles

There was a time when the days were much longer
and the years way smaller

The sun was brighter
and nothing could steal our smile

I

There once was a girl
who sat idly by, or so it seemed
With a pen in her hand
a sheet of paper in front of her
she made time her own
No one knew what she did
or how she did it
All they knew is that she *did*

Her smile was like a doe's
her lips a thin line
In the midst of everything
she had a tiger's eye:
An eye for power
An eye for success
An eye that everyone desired
that knew the future, past and present
An eye that exceeded time everywhere

Her stare shook the mountains
her blink made the water churn cold
Yet through this engulfing power
Not a sound escaped her
her thoughts were crystal clear
When she walked
Every path was a highway
Nothing stopped her
Nothing made her pause

Remember
she had the tiger's eye:

An eye brighter than a diamond
An eye filled with liquid gold
An eye as brilliant as the sun
An eye that warped time
and made it whole

Little Star

I don't want to lean on you
I want to stand
on my own two feet

I want to be able to see
the brightness of the stars
feel the tingle of the cool air

So that when I look at you
I can recognize the same light
burning passionately inside me

I Keep Working

Looking through the shadows of my room
I realize the immense demand for light
As the clock chimes nine, the need ignites

My pen moves in my hand
as my thoughts circle in my head
without this rush, my work would not be ahead

This feeling is unreal, as there is fear
and uncertainty in between
I do not know what this is called

But I know it is helping me

Time does not stop
it just keeps racing without waiting
for anyone or anything

The light never does come
and the darkness is overwhelming
but I keep working, I do not stop

My breath is shallow, my mind
is trapped, and I do not know what to do
but to keep working

My eyelids are heavy
and a yawn escapes me
instead of stopping, I keep working

I just keep working.

Inspo

I look at you
my golden light
like a speck of dust
under your warm smile
I stand at a distance
you may not see me
you may not know me
but in some way or another
in some distant time
some dream, some moment
I know we have met

Late Night Drives

I just want to drive
with the moon shining above
the wind kissing my brows

Your laugh embracing the space between
music lighting the midnight sky
just you, I and the moment

LED

The bright lights surround me
while the silence
wraps around me

The blue light does not worry me
sleep doesn't tire me
and the next day's load doesn't bury me

So carefree and young
at that moment
I am

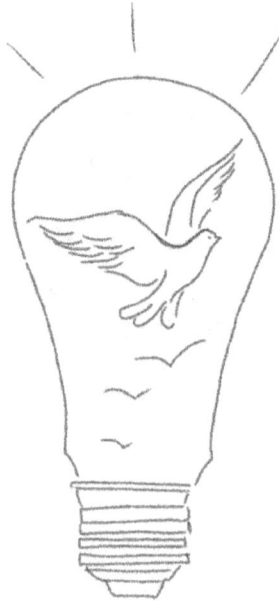

Home

Home is nomadic
it is not concrete

Neither is it wood
but a theory

An age, ever-changing
and with no boundaries

You just have to wait
and find *them*

Take Me

Sometimes
I just want to get lost in my dreams
where hopes and goals are the sidewalks
love is the skyscrapers
and laughter is the air

Success Is My Name

Raging clouds fill raven colored sky
engulfing the light inside my eyes
desperation filling my head
without hope I shall dread

Once the sun had covered magnolia branches
not a word of despair
yet the world had turned repulsive
too hard to bear

With the color of blue that fills my heart
my dear mother has said
Nothing will happen
everything's gonna be fine

Still the tears that I shed
the melancholy that rises
become discouragement instead

The light is fading, the room dimming
Sigh. Will it be true?
Will there ever be light? I wonder

Maybe, maybe not
up and down, through curves and turns
and obstacles that face my way

I force myself to have hope
because failure is not an option
and success is what I will claim

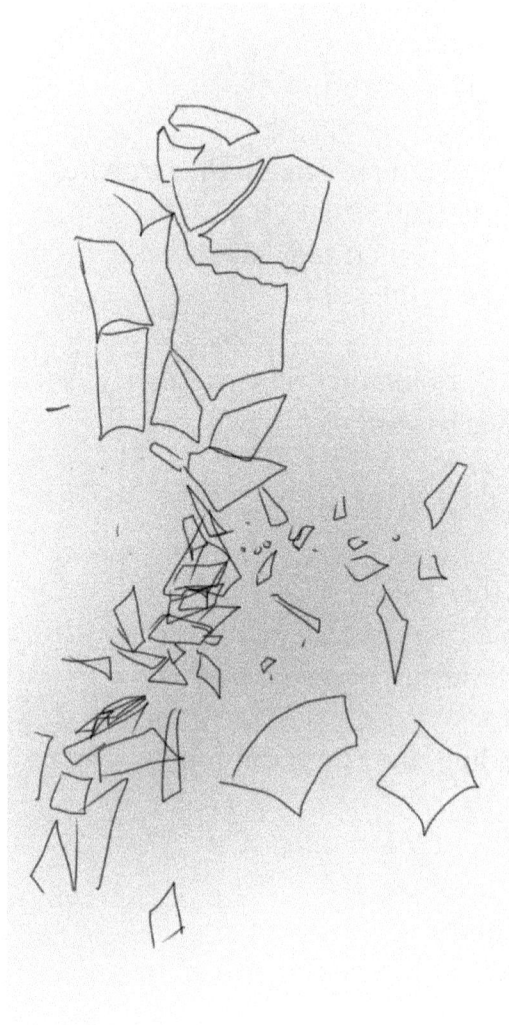

14

II.
Dusk

China Plates

They look at you as if you are nothing
like a piece of clay
ready to be made into something

You are not a person
you are a tool
you are meant for show

You are meant for their pride
and if you break
 it is certain
you will be thrown out

You must be perfect
like the china plates on the curio
you must shine

You must be perfect
they said
no flaws are allowed

Novel

We forever wait to turn the next page
until that page means nothing
and we realize the words we missed
the steps we failed to take

That the page is just a reflection
of everything we missed—
we see, but don't feel
the good years lost between those lines

Prized Possession

Plant a seed
it grows
uses everything to feel the sun
to be a part of this world

It searches the earth
to learn
to find its light
to find its firm floor

So proud it becomes
when it blooms its delicious gold
swaying brightly in the mid-summer wind
just for you to take it all

Silverscreen

We all came into this world
born in our own fitted costumes
led by our own personal agents

Each one of us a specific character
in our own epic:
don't let others direct it for you

Day Dreams

Happiness fills the tears
and tears sting our smiles

From depths we see light
while the sun caresses the night

As age becomes the young
and the young become the wise

A line so fine
with one blink

It is gone

Self Reflection

Sometimes
I just sit in the corner
dim the lights
and speak
not to another
but to myself
because at least
she sees me

Collar

I look outside the window
and see my history textbooks
I thought we were going forward
but time moved back

I see fires
I hear people's strengths
I see millions
I see ten
I see us
I see beauty
and power and love

Taken by its collar
time runs

Levers

Helping someone up
requires you
to fall down first

Phases

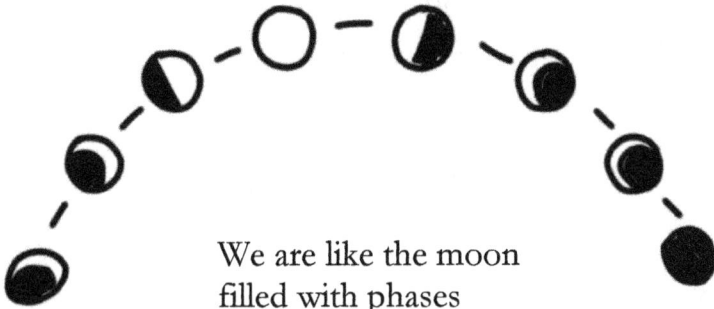

We are like the moon
filled with phases

holding different shapes
changing ourselves

only to come back
and start again

Milky Way

Your heart is your world
built with love and perspiration

Don't give it to those
who don't treat it like their universe

Trail

You are a reason for me
as I am for you

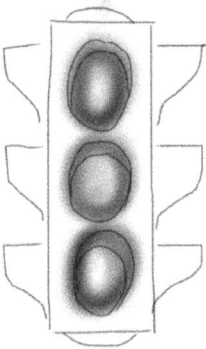

From the biscuits at the coffee shop
to unwrapping the silver wrapper
of the sweet caramel candy
every turn, left or right
has made me, has made you
arrive at this signal
and now, whether green or red
it is one we must follow

Held by the hands
of the glistening wonders above
we each follow the trail
trusting each step to be the right one
like this, we continue
tired from the weight of love

To find the reason
to find me, to find you

Huh

I don't know
sometimes I look outside
I look in the mirror
I look inside
and the puzzle just doesn't fit

Why?

We all wish
we were that girl
that boy
that person

Why do we never smile at ourselves
in front of the mirror?
Why do we always look at that one strand of hair
that is out of place?
Why are we trained to look at the problem
when the solution is always the answer?

We never say
"I want to be myself"
we always want what she has
what he has
what that person has
We never say, "Yes, I have this"

Wonders

With a smile
we cry

With tear-filled eyes
we laugh

We yearn for warmth
when it's cold

We grow
but become so young

So why do we take a step right
to only go back left?

What is this line we walk
where water meshes to lead
and gold turns to stone?

Why is it that we reach for the sun,
but wake up with the lights off?

Broken Vase

To be able to love yourself is a gift
a talent
an ability that I wish I had

For when I see myself
I see a broken girl
with flaws etched on her cheeks

Tears brimming the red under her eyes
her desperation stained dark
for all the times she has said: "I can't"

III.
High Noon

I'm Here

I open my eyes
and I see yesterday
I see tomorrow
I see the next three months
I see night
then I see day

I hear nothing
it's just me
the sun still rises, still sets
but I don't see it
it's just me

And the same day
every day

I remember that night
I remember the food
I remember the smiles
the cheers and screams
that rose around

Ten.
Nine.
Eight.
Seven.
Six.
Five.
Four.
Three.
Two.
One.

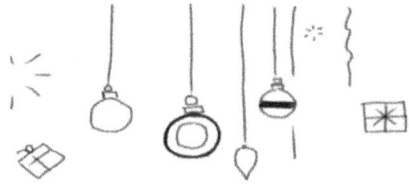

The hand of the clock shuddered
sounds of ecstasy and delight coated the air
like a soft shell around melted chocolate
holding everyone in place

What a special night!
Let's see what this year brings us!
Cheers!
Happy-Happy New Year!

Said they . . .
yet no one noticed
that the sun did not reappear

Late Nights

It's two in the morning
a shivering cool wind threatens the night
shadows spill their lies
pointing as I pass by

Indigo waves beckon me
a sharp glow above
sneering and mocking me
I try to reach for it
but a crooked smile
crosses its lips

The ground shifts beneath me
dragging me down
I try to run
but needles pierce my feet
until the shadows become light
the waves still
and my skin becomes ice

One Time Friends

I wouldn't have said *hi* three years back
I wouldn't have complimented your flower print sweater
I wouldn't have placed my bag at your table
I would have seen the *goodbye*
you were waiting to announce
I would have seen the way you started to drift by
I would have not smiled and hugged you
when clearly you were going away
I would not have missed you still

Disposable

I am not me
I am a reflection of you

A puppet, a tool
for you to use

You don't listen to me
you don't care to ask

You never have
because like plastic

You throw me
the real me, away

Headache

Needles pierce my mind
as moisture fills my eyes
knife-like tears cutting my skin

It's this mindless buzz
where the more I move
the worse it gets
The more I cry
the harder it preys
a throb that steals my thoughts

It plunders my sight
burdens me down
until the sting in my throat is too much

And I fall

Blank

Walls surround me
the sound of broken glass filling inside
the air, a heavy weight around me
a dizzying haze in sight

My breath slows
I gasp for air
I scream for help
but no one is there

Tears sting my eyes
like spears piercing my mind
I try and I try
but the air is like lead

The walls suffocate
the sounds blur
until everything
goes blank

Dear Mother

With your beauty
I grew up
your burning love became my mind

Your never stopping need to give
shaping my future
your forever laugh warming my soul

Oh dear Mother
why have you changed?
Why do your eyes fill with the cries
of a thousand pains now?

Why do your tears
stain the lands of the future?
Was this the mistake
of my childhood?

Was this your way of punishing
the branches that my brother stole away?
Oh why dear mother? What has changed?

Please forgive me, dear Mother
steal away the coldness
give back the warmth
come back, my dear Mother

Nightmare

At the end of the day
it's just a dream

The greens turn to grays
and the blues turn to black

The sweet prairie disappears
and the cheerful laughing lilies grow hemlock

A creeping wind chokes the air
an aching weight of a thousand years

Words of sweet venom cage my breath
and cold expectations grip my wrist

Until coal jade eyes fill inside

IV.
Daybreak

The Same But Not the Same

I close my eyes
and think about the little girl
I see her pigtails, I see her smile
her glasses crooked as she runs

I see her reading her books
swinging from the playground swings
I see the peace that surrounds her
the blissful ignorance that embodies her

I hear her laugh
a sound of a fresh summer day
crisp and pure
against the rustle of the mid-morning breeze

But then I see another girl
I see her pigtails, but I don't see her smile
I see her swinging
but I can't hear her laugh

She reads the same books
and follows the laughing girl
skipping and running
just the way she does

She is her truest friend
I look at this girl
and realize
we are the same

Lane

Walking down the road
I see a tree in the distance
the sky blue and taunting
the warm air
so unfamiliar against my neck

I turn to my shadows
to the room with the colored walls
the phone with those songs
the torn notebooks across the desk
the worn out shoes on the deck

I close my eyes
breathe in the new scent
and start walking
until salt encrusts my lips
and the road blurs into the tree

Runs

We question where time goes
we don't see it
but feel it pass by

We see it in our faces
our thoughts
but it never stops by with a *hello*

It pushes us
and runs away
never looking back to see if we fell

Go Back

Who are you?
Why do you remind me of the tea
cold and empty in the chipped mug?
Who are you?
What do you know about the little drawings
across my page?
Who are you?
How do you know my thoughts?
Who are you?
Will you be here . . . when I come back?

Gift Exchange

We are our own little Christmas presents
meaningful and beautiful

Filled with the love and kindness of our nurture
waiting to be let out into our world

Photograph

I look back

I remember them
I see their laughs
I hear their smiles
I remember the risks
I remember the despair
I remember the times

The colors bleed out
and the pixels fade
until nothing is visible
and nothing remains

I hear the whispers
but no one is there
I look outside
but no one is there

I look back at the photograph
to find only the blank card left
the fading lines of their smiles
buried in time

A memory was all it was

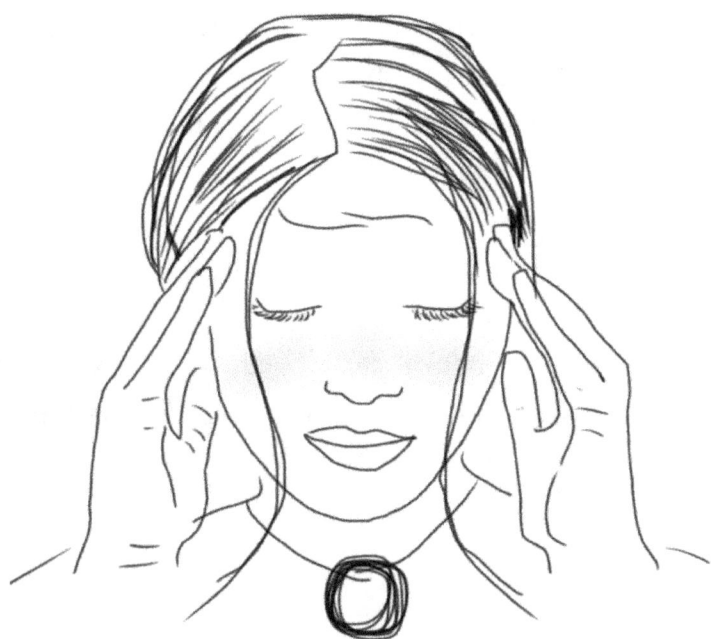

Acknowledgments

With deep appreciation and love, I would like to thank my dad, Bikramaditya Mukherjee, for supporting me throughout the writing process.

I would like to thank my little brother, Adhrit Mukherjee, for helping me organize my thoughts and encouraging me at every moment.

I would like to offer my special thanks and gratitude to my mother, Lopamudra Mukherjee, who inspired my love for writing and reading poetry.

Thank you to my friends and loved ones for believing in me.

And special thanks to my editor and publisher, Karen Mireau Rimmer, for her amazing skill, vision and thought in making this all come to life!

About the Author

Kriti Mukherjee was born in 2003 in Kolkata, West Bengal, India. She moved to the United States in 2009 and has lived in six states and has visited forty others since childhood.

Kriti has always displayed an immense love for art, working in oil, charcoal and pencil. She has shown her portraits, landscapes, and thematic pieces in school exhibitions and is involved in the local arts community.

She has also immersed herself in a variety of literary pursuits—from writing short stories in her elementary years to developing meaningful poems as she got older.

Through her poems, Kriti expresses the vulnerability of being an adolescent girl in the face of expectations set by family, friends and society. Her simple words depict the nostalgia, pain, self loathing, hope and beauty that comes from being a teenager in the 21st century.

Kriti currently lives in Princeton, New Jersey, with her mother, father, and younger brother. This is her first full-length collection of poems.

To contact the Author:

Instagram: @kriti.mukherjee12
Gmail: kritimukherjee12@gmail.com
Facebook: https://www.facebook.com/kriti.mukherjee.5
Twitter: @KritiMukherjee12

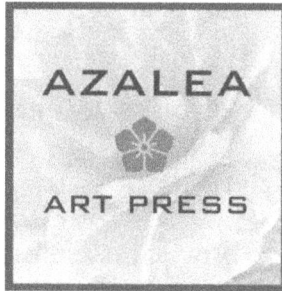

To contact the Publisher:

please email:
Azalea.Art.Press@gmail.com
https://azaleaartpress.blogspot.com